Career
Perspectives in
Student
Affairs

Edited By:

Alan F. Kirby
Director
University Center
University of California at Santa Barbara

Dudley Woodard
Vice President for Student Affairs
University of Arizona

Volume I; NASPA Monograph Series
Published By The National Association
of Student Personnel Administrators, Inc.

Printed in U.S.A.

Career Perspectives in Student Affairs. Copyright 1984 by The National Association of Student Personnel Administrators. Printed and bound in the United States of America. All rights reserved. No part of this book may be reproduced in any form or by any electronic or mechanical means including information storage and retrieval systems without permission in writing from the publisher, except by a reviewer who may quote brief passages in a review. First edition.

Library of Congress Cataloging in Publication Data
Main entry under title:
Career perspectives in student affairs.
    Bibliography: p.
    1. Student counselors—Vocational guidance—United States—Addresses, essays, lectures. 2. Personnel service in higher education—United States—Addresses, essays, lectures. I. Kirby, Alan F., 1951- . II. Woodard, Dudley, 1940- . III. National Association of Student Personnel Administrators (U.S.)
LB2343.C3276 1984   378'.194   84-2006
ISBN 0-931654-01-7

Foreword

The idea of this publication first came up during a meeting of the National Association of Student Personnel Administrators (NASPA), Division of Career Development and Placement (CD&P), in 1976. In that meeting the CD&P members had enjoyed a discussion of how they had come to careers in student affairs, of the complexities of making choices for personal and professional development, and of advice they wished they had received from, or would like to give to, others in the field. From that lively discussion came a strong urge to develop a manuscript along the lines of the conversation just concluded. Thus began the production planning of *Career Perspectives in Student Affairs*.

Authors were identified and contracted, manuscripts were drafted and subjected to editorial revisions. But even as the writing and editing began, the CD&P Division, and NASPA itself, were changing. CD&P merged with the Division of Professional Development and Standards (PD&S) to become the Division of Career Development and Professional Standards (CD&PS), and took on new and expanded responsibilities. NASPA added the Division of Communication Services, including a monograph editor and monograph board, to be responsible for all publications.

Finding its way through these organization changes, the product of the 1976 discussion first emerged in 1981 as a spiral-bound, limited-edition monograph distributed to members of the NASPA board of directors and members of the 1976-81 divisions. Now, thanks to the efforts of the monograph board, and especially editor David Meabon, the encouragement of the NASPA board of directors, and the funds from the NASPA Institute of Research and Development (NIRAD), this revised manuscript has come to publication in 1984.

As one of the few NASPA officers to have been involved with this project from idea to publication, I am particularly pleased to see *Career Perspectives in Student Affairs* added to the list of NASPA professional publications.

—R. Mikell O'Donnell
NASPA Past President
November 1983

Career Perspectives in Student Affairs

Careers in Student Affairs: An Introduction

by Arthur Sandeen, University of Florida

Should you consider a career in the college student affairs field? How does one enter this profession? What kinds of qualifications and training are required? What are the opportunities for growth and advancement? What are the satisfactions and rewards? What are the major problems and issues involved? Just what is student affairs all about?

These are the questions that this monograph is designed to address; it is directed to persons thinking about student affairs as a possible career, and to those already in the field who may be concerned about their career futures. The monograph is very personal in its approach, as the authors feel that career decisions, especially in this field, are not made in a detached, mechanical manner. The authors are all successful practitioners, representing various levels of experience, and they share their personal perspective with the reader.

This monograph presents no orderly theory of occupational choice, few statistics from scientific studies, and no data that will magically reveal whether to enter (or remain in) this field. The authors recognize that the process of career choice is extremely complex and feel that this monograph may assist those considering the student affairs profession because of its personal approach. It is hoped that it will stimulate discussion among students and staff on campuses and at regional and national meetings.

A Brief Look at Our History

"Student affairs" has evolved into a very diverse field over the years, and those working in it are involved in a wide range of activities. When the student affairs field began around the turn of the century, this was not the case. At that time, the increasing size, complexity, and residential nature of many colleges caused some presidents to appoint a person to "look after the students" and attend to academic advising, personal, housing, and conduct matters. The early deans were appointed from among the ranks of the faculty, and essentially created their own responsibilities.

When LeBaron Russell Briggs was appointed dean at Harvard in 1890, many of the faculty were resentful and skeptical. However, he became so popular with students and assisted so many of them that he became a legend at that institution. When Lois Kimball Mathews became dean of women at Wisconsin in 1910, she found herself facing tremendous obstacles. The faculty was virtually all male, women students were not viewed as very important, and she was granted almost no authority. Nevertheless, she became a pioneering champion of women's academic rights, established an effective student affairs program at Wisconsin, and wrote one of the best books on student affairs ever published, *The Dean of Women* (1915).

Stanley Coulter's situation at Purdue was not very different. Upon being appointed dean he wrote a letter to the board, asking them to describe his duties and responsibilities. The board replied to Dean Coulter that it had no idea, *but that he should get on with the job immediately!* These early deans provided assistance to students on a face-to-face basis, had no real staff, and operated on personality. They handled almost every conceivable problem of students.

It was at this time that applied psychology came into being and found expression in the vocational guidance movement. The interest in individual differences was greatly stimulated by the measurement advances made during the testing of recruits for World War I. It was only logical for this movement to be extended to the colleges, and as a result admissions, registration, academic advising, counseling, and placement programs were established to assist students. William Rainey Harper of Chicago spoke for the "scientific study of the college student," and colleges sought new ways to meet the needs of their students (Harper, 1950).

The history of American higher education has consistently reflected controversy over what the undergraduate curriculum should be. In many ways, the student affairs field and its emergence as a profession have been part of that controversy. Even though most colleges were small (the University of Michigan's enrollment was 700 in 1895), there was great concern over the rapidly developing departmentalization and professionalization of knowledge, as influenced by the German universities. In criticizing American higher education, J.H. Muirhead (1910), a philosophy professor and president of the Froebel Society, stated the following:

> Our college curriculum is agglutinative. It is like a department store, with a few bargain counters. We have added subjects with every new turn of affairs . . . the institutions are like factories running with a full force in the effort to turn out the largest number of marketable products. The colleges are busy imparting facts and scarcely remember there is any distinction between information, knowledge, and wisdom.

Those early deans in student affairs positions were part of an effort to bring wholeness to the college experience, to bridge the gap between the curriculum and student life, and to make the institution more humane. This situation, of course, continues on most campuses today.

As the need for student affairs programs on campuses increased, professional associations were formed, national conferences were held, training programs were established, standards of practice were developed, and a literature began to emerge.

New services and programs appeared on the campuses, reflecting advances in the field, the expectations of students and their parents, and of course, changes in the world. Student government, student organizations, intercollegiate and intramural sports, student health, and residence halls, all were in need of personnel to establish and supervise these new programs. During the very difficult depression years of the 1930s, the natural emphasis in student affairs was in counseling, advising, student employment, and placement.

The post-World War II period saw the greatest and most rapid expansion of higher education in American history. As enrollments exploded, emphasis in the country was placed upon increased access, and a much higher proportion of young people wanted to attend college. Again, with increasing numbers of students, the student affairs profession continued to expand, and an institution's "division of student affairs" often consisted of several large departments, coordinated and directed by people who had received extensive professional training in the field. The student affairs field became highly specialized during the 1950s, and each specialty formed its own professional association, set of standards, professional journal, national meetings, and literature. Thus the registrar, the foreign student adviser, the residence hall counselor, the placement director, the Counseling Center counselor, the intramural sports adviser, the student health director, the Greek organization adviser, and the dean each had a separate identity. This rapid proliferation and specialization of functions became a matter of concern and controversy, and several attempts to coordinate and even merge some of these groups have been made during the past twenty-five years. The efforts have not succeeded; in fact, the number of new specialties and organizations has increased!

The forces at work in American society during the 1950s and 1960s were clearly reflected on the nation's campuses, and again the student affairs field adjusted to the changes. The emphasis upon civil rights found expression in new codes of student conduct and official statements of student freedoms. Student affairs staffs assumed the leadership in handling student disturbances during the Vietnam war, and helped to create new ways for students to participate in institutional policy decision. The Congress of the United States decided that no one should be denied access to college because of a lack of money, and massive financial aid programs were established. These programs were administered on campuses by student affairs personnel.

Student Affairs Today

In the past few years, the decline of the birth rate, the women's movement, and consumer protection interests have had an impact upon the activities of student affairs professionals. Increased competition for students has created greatly expanded programs in admissions, orientation, and retention. Larger numbers of older, nontraditional students (mostly women) entering higher education have stimulated additional services and programs developed by student affairs personnel. The concept of "student as consumer" has emerged as an effort to emphasize fair practices on the part of institutions in the recruitment of students and in the delivery of stated educational programs.

In the late 1950s, the total enrollment in American higher education was less than 3 million students. (In 1980, this figure was over 11 million.) Community colleges were established in record numbers during this time, and student affairs staffs have been an important part of these institutions from their beginning. No country in history has ever before experienced anything like the growth in higher education that the United States experienced during this period. The student affairs field expanded in a similar manner, and it has now become established as one of the major components of virtually all institutions, along with academic affairs, business affairs, and institutional development. Despite the many problems in higher education, the student affairs field has never been stronger than it is today, and the largest number of highly trained people in our history are now practicing in a great variety of positions. The total number of professionally trained staff working in student affairs during the past twenty-five years has more than tripled.

Because of the stabilization of enrollments, the rapid expansion in new positions for faculty and student affairs personnel has diminished in the past five years. Moreover, mobility of per-

sonnel among institutions has decreased because of compara-
tively low turnover in positions and the high cost of moving.
Thus, after an unparalleled period of growth, higher education
now faces an uncertain future. This has caused great concern in
most of the academic professions, and student affairs is no exception. Young people wonder if it is a good decision to begin
graduate studies in the field if their career opportunities may be
limited.

Entry-level and middle-management staff in student affairs
may be experiencing frustration over their inability to advance
as rapidly as they know they might have in the 1950s and 1960s.
Those in administrative positions may tire of the increased pressures, and may experience "burn-out," with few other career
options available to them. While these conditions are not at all
unique to student affairs, there is real concern about the consequences of the uncertain situation for the future of the field, for
higher education, and for the students. The concern has led to
an unprecedented interest in professional development programs, discussion about careers at national conferences, and
publications such as this one.

The student affairs field, since its very inception, has attracted people with a strong sense of service to others. While
graduate training programs have become quite specialized and
sophisticated, the basic needs for service and human compassion have remained unchanged. The career options for persons
wanting to enter this field are now marvelously diverse, both in
terms of job function and type of institution. A partial list of actual current job titles of student affairs professionals at selected
institutions illustrates this fact:

Dean of Students
Recreation Specialist
Financial Aid Counselor
Minority Student Adviser
Registrar
Residence Hall Counselor
Placement Director
Student Union Director

Director of Student Employment
Orientation Coordinator
Foreign Student Adviser
Handicapped Student Adviser
Mature Student Adviser
Student Government Adviser
Director of Leadership Development
Intramurals Director
Student Health Educator
Transfer Admissions Specialist
Mental Health Specialist
Director of Student Affairs Research
Adviser to Greek Organizations
College Counselor
Coordinator of Religious Affairs
Educational Opportunity Program Director
Cooperative Education Director
Director of Athletics
Director of Recruitment and Retention
Crisis Center Coordinator
Director of Student Judicial Affairs
Student Organizations Adviser
Director of Housing
Coordinator of Nontraditional Student Services
Director of Veteran Affairs

Such a list of specialists would have seemed unthinkable to Dean Briggs or Dean Mathews only seventy years ago. In addition to the great variety of positions now in existence, there is a much greater variety of institutions. Among the 3,000 colleges and universities that employ student affairs staff are graduate research universities, private church-related colleges, urban commuter colleges, service academies, professional schools, and theological seminaries. Depending upon skills and experience, student affairs trained staff may also work in community service agencies, government service programs, human development programs in business and industry, or as consultants to these agencies.

Surviving and Growing in the Future

As one studies the history of the student affairs field, perhaps the most impressive characteristic of the profession that emerges is its ability to adapt to the changing needs of students, institutions, and society. As issues and problems have appeared, new services and programs have been developed by student affairs staff. The profession has often assumed a leadership role in institutional change.

Student affairs leaders fought for increased opportunities for women students long before such activity became popular; established fair procedures in the handling of student conduct cases before legalistic practices were thrust upon institutions, insisted upon equal access for minority students in campus activities before the civil rights movement, initiated drug education programs before colleges wanted to recognize that there was a problem, and stated the case for student freedoms on the campus during the great turmoil of the 1960s.

The student affairs profession has established ethical standards, statements on good practice, and standards by which effective programs can be evaluated, and has recommended standards for professional training programs. There are many excellent journals, monographs, national conference reports, and an extensive and growing literature. However, there is no static body of knowledge constituting this field that is merely passed on to the next generation of professionals.

The successful career student affairs professional is one who understands the difficulties facing higher education, knows the history of the profession, is able to adapt to changing issues and problems, and can organize people and resources around these matters to address the problems effectively. Any alert professional working in the field today is aware of the many problems and needs that institutions and students have. If the student affairs field is to remain a dynamic force on the campuses, it must assume an active leadership role in addressing such problems. That is how we have arrived at our current position of strength, and it is how we must move ahead from here.

Perhaps as much as any existing profession, the student affairs field embodies the concept of service to others. Because people working in this field are in almost constant contact with students, whose role it is to learn, there are additional responsibilities beyond the mere job functions that are performed. Student affairs professionals teach students about careers largely by how they handle their own in the eyes of students. Students need to learn that while a career in some field is essential, they have personal identities and worth as people apart from their careers. Student affairs professionals need to help students understand the differences between a job and a career, and the possible negative consequences of assisting all of their ego need fulfillment with the attainment of a certain position. The most effective student affairs professional is rarely the superdedicated fanatic who elevates every issue to the level of a crisis; it is the honest, clear-thinking individual who retains a healthy perspective on campus problems and remains sensitive to student needs.

The student affairs profession can be an exciting and stimulating love affair with students, ideas, and higher education. Above all, it demands that we serve other people with humaneness and compassion. The functions and services that student affairs professionals have provided on college campuses for many years are essential in the American higher education system. With the increasing diversity of our colleges and of the students enrolled in them, the challenges for student affairs are more exciting than ever before. The promise of this profession is that it provides a real opportunity to serve. The potential is unlimited!

Preparing for Student Personnel in the 1980s

by Robert H. Shaffer, Indiana University

The title of this chapter may well have been "Preparing for the Unknown—Student Personnel Work in the 1980s" or, positively but more conservatively, "Preparing for Ambiguity and Change—Student Personnel Work in the 1980s." The emphasis in such titles would probably express the significance of the chapter content, as differentiated from the content a reader would normally expect. Some readers would expect to find a list of courses that should be completed and a description of the degree to be obtained as sort of a union card. Other readers might expect a list of competencies and traits that student personnel workers should possess. Still other readers would expect a discussion of the work of student personnel workers, their goals, problems, and challenges, and suggestions for preparing to avoid predicted pitfalls and problems.

All of these expectancies are justified, and certainly any potential staff member in the field needs such information. However, except for gross generalities, it is practically impossible to present such information in a meaningful, applicable manner in the space of a few short pages. Articles and books in the suggested reading list at the end of this monograph, chosen from scores of possibilities, indicate the breadth of the topic and the complexity of summarizing it meaningfully. Of all the preparation programs for the professional, those for preparing student personnel workers are among the most difficult to define in traditional terms. Student personnel functions are performed in a great variety of institutional settings, within a broad range of administrative structures, by individuals who came to their positions along many different paths and with varied experiences. Added to these facts is the additional characteristic of rapid change as a dominant feature of current and future higher education.

The Environment of Higher Education in the 1980s

Most colleges and universities currently face very tight financial situations caused by inflation, student enrollment declines in many fields, and competition for funds with other agencies and social needs. Frequently these budget crunches are accompanied by the need to initiate or broaden certain types of student services such as those for older, handicapped, part-time, and minority students, who have often been neglected in the past. One of the major challenges facing student personnel administrators in the current environment of higher education is *how to do more with less.* A related series of trends and forces is causing the value, propriety or need of some traditional services to be challenged with such questions as: Should the college provide assistance to the student in locating housing off-campus and in dealing with landlords? Should student activities be provided for students by institutional staff, or should they be left to students to initiate, fund, and conduct? How much counseling is really necessary and defensible on a bare-bones or survival budget? How much money should be expended in enforcing rules and disciplinary codes? These are merely suggestive of the types of questions that are being asked today and that will be asked with greater intensity in the years immediately ahead.

Many of the current student personnel programs have their

roots in an era when the typical college was residential, relatively isolated, and committed to almost total concern for student life. Many students today attend college as commuters, part-time while employed, or as relatively anonymous individuals in urban settings. Even on traditional college campuses there has been a growing legal relationship between the institution and the student that emphasizes the adulthood and autonomy of the individual and the safeguarding of consumer and civil rights. These developments in many instances are making the traditionally conceived all-encompassing educational relationship obsolete.

Further complicating the scene for which student personnel workers are preparing is the seemingly widespread feeling by the larger society that all is not well in academia. Feelings, as reported in polls, newspaper editorials, and public statements are that students are not learning the right things, that problems of drinking, drugs, immature behavior, aimlessness and confusion regarding vocational and educational goals, together with cheating and athletic scandals, are symptomatic of fundamental problems.

Student personnel for most of this century has received wide support, generally because it contributed to the resolution of campus problems and aided students in the formation of desirable values, development of human relations and leadership skills, establishment of sound goals and aspirations, adaptation of appropriate lifestyles, and exhibition of acceptable social behavior. Some of the questions currently being raised about student personnel ask, "What value are various student services and programs if they cannot contribute in a positive, demonstrable way to student growth and development?"

Preparation for Student Personnel Positions

From the preceding cursory review of some of the characteristics of present-day academia and its problems, it is evident that *preparing for positions in student personnel must be a continuous, ongoing process,* whether by individuals new to the field and hoping to enter it or by staff members retreading for different positions or institutional settings. If change is one of the dominant characteristics of higher education, then staff members of colleges and universities will be required more than ever before to work with change in individuals and institutions.

Most professional fields require periodic if not continuous updating. Various professional associations and certifying agencies make periodic updating a requirement to remain in good standing. Student personnel, through its professional associations may move in that direction in the near future. It requires from its professionals so many different skills to be exercised in so many diverse settings that no one period of preparation can possibly prepare an individual for a long period of time, let alone a professional career spanning many years.

The demands of student personnel positions for adaptable and flexible staff members who find it rewarding to work in ambiguous, often unstructured relationships to individuals and groups point out the "good news—bad news" dilemma of present-day higher education. The bad news is that it is not clear how the economic, political, and social upheavals that appear to be characterizing the decade of the 1980s will impinge upon postsecondary education. Budget stringencies, no-growth or even contracting situations, demands for cost effectiveness, and drastic reassessment of traditional assumptions all combine to shake traditional fields and individuals engaged in them. Anxiety, tension, insecurity, and even personal and professional self-doubt may result.

The good news is that the same forces offer unusual opportunities for creative leadership and significant contributions to one of society's essential enterprises—the education of its people. Public opinion polls and expressions of leaders in our society show that few people question the fundamental worth of higher education. Most agree that our future is bleak indeed unless we prepare our most talented people for leadership in an era of change. Higher education is in a strong position to respond to the challenge. In turn, student personnel, as a significant subsystem of the higher-education general system, will have wide support if it produces the values it claims for its work. Thus, there are unusual opportunities for student personnel workers skilled in conceptualizing, initiating, and interpreting programs and services designed to meet the problems faced in the 1980s.

For these reasons, personal and professional preparation of individuals for careers in student affairs in higher education consists of much more than formal courses, attaining a degree, or even just mastering skills necessary to gain employment in entry level positions. More importantly, the preparation must include *attention to an individual's own life goals, self-image, personal aspirations, standards, and motivations* in addition to the usually expected thorough grounding in professional theory and competencies. The field is broad and diverse and must be staffed by individuals with wide ranges and variations in their backgrounds and training. New points of view and new ways of looking at old problems will be in demand on every staff.

New Skills Needed

Specific staff and institutional needs vary widely. However, in the field as a whole there are some skills and abilities that currently seem to be in particular demand. One area is the application of computer technology to various aspects of student affairs. Most current staff directors entered the field before the expansion of computer science and electronic communication. Thus, they need to recruit new members of their staffs who are skilled not only in working with computer specialists but also in initiating and applying basic computer skills and knowledge to functions in student affairs. Every individual completing a preparation program currently and in the future would do well to acquire a basic understanding of computer applications for university administration.

Another area that has expanded in recent years is that of evaluation, student and institutional needs assessment, and research. Traditionally, student affairs has been primarily reactive to events and responsive to demands. In fact, student affairs administrators have been described as characteristically racing from fire to fire, rather than serving as early warning officials leading the way in planning innovation. Evaluation, as a technical field, has made enormous strides in the 1970s, and new professionals will be wise to be skilled in the new approaches, procedures, and content in this area.

The fact that student affairs, along with all other subsystems of higher education, will face strong requirements of *accountability* in the years immediately ahead suggests another skill area holding strong attraction for new professionals. (The demands themselves are not particularly new; the need to be expert in the area *is* new.) Student affairs has always been accountable to a wide range of critical publics. Faculty, administrators, parents, students, townspeople, alumni, and the media have applied to student affairs some of the toughest, most rigorous criteria for accountability ever faced by an enterprise. What is new is the need for staff members in the field to be skilled in demonstrating and interpreting the worth of a program, service, or function long before the direct question of worth is asked.

Thus, skills in communication, public relations (viewed broadly), relating to special constituencies in the institutional context, and interacting with various publics are of particular importance in the current environment of higher education. Also, cost principles of higher education must be understood along with basic accounting principles that will be applicable to the specifics of a department operation or to understanding broader issues. The student affairs professional must understand the costs of education and how those costs are determined in order to better communicate and account for educational needs.

In addition to the specialized skills discussed above, it is also essential for new staff members in any of the traditional functional areas to be able to work in the broadest possible context. For example, student activities will often be total-campus or even total-community programs; counselors will be required to work with institutional and community mental health agencies; housing will encompass all types of options; orientation will need to appeal to a wide spectrum of clientele. Thus, regardless of the particular specialties that individuals preparing for careers in student affairs may choose, it is important to prepare for the application and practice of those specialties in the widest context. Adaptability and breadth of view are more likely to determine for specific individuals what fields are open to them in student affairs than a mere survey of the professional positions themselves.

Despite the needed wide variation in individual characteristics and the broad range of institutional settings, the individuals working in the field and the institutions within which they will be working have much in common. Individuals working in the student affairs field, at whatever level or specific function, must be committed to the educational, social, and economic goals of assisting others to develop to their highest potential. The pursuit of higher education is a rigorous, demanding activity. Providing programs and services to assist students at any age and of almost any background to succeed requires commitment, expertise, and ingenuity. Life in academia can be threatening, frightening, discouraging, often impersonal, and lonely. Student programs and services in a variety of ways assist individuals in setting and progressing toward their life goals. The student development point of view, which possesses many more complex aspects than those stated here, is basic to successful work in student affairs.

Institutions of higher education are committed to teaching, research, and service. The balance between these functions varies widely from one institutional type to another, but all types are committed to the academic enterprise, to the pursuit of knowledge, and to the development of skills in their students. If all students were alike, the need for student services would be lessened. However, few students are even superficially alike. Even in apparently homogeneous student bodies there are wide variations in interests, aspirations, values, motivation, physical development, and intellectual maturity. It is the function of student affairs to help academic institutions meet the widely varied needs of their individual students and to assist them in utilizing total institutional resources effectively.

At one time in the development of the student personnel field it was often stated that student programs and services existed to care for the out-of-class needs of students so they could be successful in their class work. That (now obsolete) view failed to recognize the fact that all individuals live, grow, and develop twenty-four hours a day, seven days a week, and not just during the relatively few hours that they are engaged in formal academic activities. Therefore, there is a need for a part of the institution to focus specifically upon the integration of all aspects of the institutional environment into a coherent educational force.

An important aspect of current educational thought under-lies the need for student programs and services in academia. That is the recognition that *effective education results from an individual's own motivation and interests.* Whether education is the content of courses or the attitudes, values, and aspirations formed, it cannot be externally imposed upon students against their will by sheer force of academic authority. For this reason, student personnel workers are required to work closely with professorial colleagues in conveying to students the image of self-directing individuals utilizing the institution's resources to prepare themselves to achieve self-established goals.

The Nature of the Preparation Program

From the foregoing description of some aspects of the role of student personnel in higher education in the 1980s, it can be seen that there can be no one method of preparing future staff members. So much depends upon the personal interests, concerns, aspirations, and experiences that the potential newcomer to the field brings to the training program. It is generally recognized that any program for educating the student personnel professional must combine a sound basis of theory with supervised practice based upon the student's personal characteristics and experiences. Thus, from the individual student's point of view, a program must be individually tailored to immediate and long-range personal and professional goals.

The early work of the Council of Student Personnel Associations in Higher Education (COSPA), acting through an interassociation commission on the professional preparation of student personnel workers, divided the content of training programs into *substantive knowledge, skills, and techniques.* In its report, substantive knowledge included such topics as the nature of the college student, colleges and social institutions, counseling principles and techniques, administration, group work, and the history, theory, and nature of student personnel as a field.

Subsequent writing, especially that emanating from the American College Personnel Association's (ACPA) Tomorrow's Higher Education project, added an emphasis upon human development, learning, and organizational theories, and particularly upon assessment and evaluation.

The area of skills and techniques in the early COSPA report (1964) included competencies associated with individual assessment, goal setting, and change processes as applied to three different types of clientele: (1) individuals, (2) groups, and (3) organizations in three categories of roles: administrators, instructors, or consultants. Using this conceptual approach, the COSPA Commission's 1972 report included a three-dimensional model illustrating twenty-seven different skills, as utilized in working with the three types of clientele in the roles of administrators, instructors, and consultants, using skills grouped in the three compentency areas.

Later writing (Peterson, 1977; Arner *et al.*, 1976) has emphasized *personal and individual development* as essential outcomes of any professional training program. In light of the current and predicted environment of higher education, the development of one's own personal and professional identity has been emphasized (see Arner *et al.*, 1976, for a more complete list).

Individuals attempting to investigate the nature and content of training programs face a difficult task because of the practical impossibility of discerning the content of courses from their titles, or of perceiving the nature of practical experiences without knowing the quality of supervision and amount of discussion accompanying the experiences. Some programs emphasize theoretical courses more than others. Some emphasize administration of student services as opposed to the intensive development of a specialty in a functional area. Others emphasize counseling as the basic approach to the field. Still others emphasize process and experience as opposed to traditional academic approaches.

Differences in content, dominant emphasis, and prevailing orientation may be discernible in program descriptions or through interviewing faculty members. Often, however, these differences are entirely obscured by traditional generalities, token attention to key areas, or even internal unawareness of the actual nature and characteristics of specific programs.

Perhaps the most useful general statement that can be made

regarding the selection of a preparation program by a prospective graduate student is: *Analyze the program structure and content as thoroughly as possible in preparation for interviews with one or more faculty members and with students and graduates of the program under consideration.* Most programs issue lists of their graduates and where they are working. While job titles vary greatly and often are as ambiguous and indefinite as course titles, jobs held by graduates may give an indication of the major program emphasis. Relating a program's offerings to one's own purposes, self-assessment of need and of personal and professional goals is not only essential to securing the most value from the effort involved but also is fundamental to establishing a sound basis for a professional career.

In view of the many changes predicted for higher education in general and student personnel in particular, it seems wise for a newcomer entering the field to view initial formal preparation as primarily a broad base for a lifelong career that might lead into a number of specialties or areas of work. Thus, ascertaining what flexibility there is in a particular program's requirements is an essential step before any decision regarding application is made. If the predictions are true that change, ambiguity, and tight budgets will characterize higher education in the decade ahead, then consideration must be given to developing interests, learning skills, and building a knowledge base in a number of functional areas.

Even more than currently, future institutional situations will require combinations of specialties for work in a number of functional areas at the same time. For example, if recruitment and retention of students will be emphasized along with the energetic assessment of personnel, the evaluation of programs, and the reallocation of resources to meet new and emerging needs, then the student currently in a preparation program should strive to become skilled in areas contributing to such processes.

Those individuals already in the field in entry- or middle-level positions are at particularly critical stages in their professional careers. Two or three years of just performing a function the way it has always been performed at a given institution or the way it was taught in a given training program may make an individual less productive, and therefore less valuable to a staff, than a newly graduated person. The latter, just emerging from an up-to-date preparation program emphasizing such topics as program and policy evaluation, organizational development, computer application of student data, and budgeting processes, could be able to make a more significant contribution. Thus, the individual on the job, just as an individual in initial training, must be especially alert to learning new concepts and skills in addition to basic theory and traditional practices.

Formal or informal internal staff development programs are not just visible evidences of strong leadership and sound professional work, they are essential to personal and professional survival in an era of rapid change. Staff members need to implement their own development programs if they should be in an institution lacking such activities.

A preparation plan for entry into the field of student personnel, or for advancement within it, must possess certain characteristics: (1) it must be developmental in nature, starting where the individual is in a particular skill, knowledge, or attitudinal area and progressing to more sophisticated and professional levels; (2) it must concern itself with the operational value system guiding the individual's own interpersonal relations and behavior in various settings; (3) it must combine learning with doing, not just for understanding, but for developing the ability to initiate new and different programs, procedures, and policies where necessary; (4) it must facilitate and stimulate an individual's reaching out to new fields of knowledge that might contribute to depth, adaptability, and discernment; (5) and finally, individual staff members must see good professional practice, in its broadest sense, as their base for security and confidence, and not just as a means of looking good to a professor in a class or supervisor on the job. The outcome of professional preparation at all levels must be constant and continuous professional and personal growth throughout life. Only individuals who are growing themselves are able to help others grow—the underlying goal of all student work.

The New Professional

by Alan F. Kirby, University of California, Santa Barbara

The intention of this chapter is to address topics relevant to *new professionals* in the student affairs area. Three groups of individuals are primarily addressed: (1) undergraduate students who are curious about this profession and wish to know more about the realities of the work involved; (2) graduate students currently in student personnel programs who want to gain a better understanding of what lies ahead after graduation; and (3) student affairs professionals in their first or second year of work who wish to gain another perspective on this stage of career development. In addition, a fourth interested group might be those managers in the field who directly supervise entry-level positions—perhaps this chapter will in some way stimulate thought about responding to the needs of new professionals as they struggle to develop their professional identities.

In Art Sandeen's chapter of this publication, a sampling of available student affairs positions was listed. The list represents only a small portion of the many different types of jobs with student affairs. The variety of potential positions for first-year people is staggering, particularly when one considers the many entry-level spots within most housing organizations (where there is a residence hall, there undoubtedly is a hall director, and where there is a hall director, there is someone destined to burn out, move on, and leave space for that next fresh face). Such is the case for many entry-level positions. Perhaps this chapter can help explain what that year is often like and how it fits in with one's career development.

Emotional Dilemmas: The Transition from Graduate School to Career Employment

Leaving the security of graduate school and entering the job market can be a tense and very anxious time for some. It can also be an exciting and challenging time, as the recent graduate seeks that very important first position. Many job seekers will travel to at least one national student personnel conference that offers a placement service. At such conferences, employers can advertise openings and job candidates can perform one of the more important sales jobs of their young lives.

The marketing of one's talents can be an arduous task for some candidates. Others, however, plunge into a placement center with courage, conviction, and an indomitable spirit. The difficult time arrives when all résumés have been submitted for positions ranging from most desired to least desired. Of course, there are a great many "acceptable," though perhaps not exciting, job listings within the range of possibility. As the waiting for interviews grows longer, those less desired positions slowly become more desirable and most candidates predictably find themselves becoming *much* more flexible regarding salary, title, and geographical location. Waiting for interviews sometimes leads to a variety of self-defeating behaviors as one begins comparing outward appearances with other candidates at the placement service. While other candidates seem to move smoothly through the area with an air of self-confidence and self-assuredness, an observer can confuse that exterior with traits of talent, competence, and experience. The nervous candidate waiting for an interview can make some false assumptions and end up with a quickly eroding sense of self-confidence. Suddenly, *everyone* seems well qualified and there are even thoughts of giving up the job search.

As time continues to go by and interview prospects seem slim, one might begin to reminisce about the good times in graduate school and the security of the academic setting. A recent graduate with a master of arts degree or a doctor of philosophy degree in hand has probably been used to being viewed as one of the older, wiser students in the department, simply by virtue of seniority. The first-year students may have turned to the more experienced student for counsel, either informally or in a more formal classroom or clinic setting in which the advanced student held a graduate assistantship. The transition from the experienced graduate student to the inexperienced new professional can be rather dramatic. Thoughts of pursuing an additional degree (or two) begin to creep into one's consciousness, but becoming a "professional student" has its emotional and financial drawbacks as well. The reality of "life after graduate school" quickly comes into focus, and for many a recent graduate, reality just might not seem too inviting!

Approaching the First Position

Even with the emotional dilemmas noted, most graduates will indeed manage to have a few interviews either at a conference or at a college or university. Unfortunately, because the atmosphere surrounding a job search can be filled with a great deal of tension, candidates can quickly lose sight of their own personal needs and values. Suddenly, the *only* consideration is to receive a job offer—*any* offer. Important questions about the breadth of responsibilities associated with the position, type of flexibility inherent in the job, and the quality of colleagues at the institution might not be asked in the excitement of those initial interviews. However, questions such as these must be asked if the candidate intends to evaluate the worth of a position comprehensively. Ed Birch, in his chapter of this publication, describes four important variables to consider when seeking a position in this profession. It would be to the new professional's advantage to pay close attention to his suggestions and to carefully analyze potential job openings using those guidelines.

Another pitfall when seeking a first position is to enter the employment market *with fixed, rigid impressions of specific positions within student affairs*. If these impressions are not founded on a great deal of experience or the judgment of respected others, they may mistakenly lead one to ignore positions that might otherwise have proved to be excellent starting points in the profession. Too many graduates enter the job market convinced that positions on other campuses will be similar, if not identical, to comparable positions on the candidate's own campus. Thus, applications are not submitted, interviews are not conducted, and individuals find themselves still hoping for the perfect position that never seems to materialize.

A highly restrictive housing position on one campus might be a flexible, innovative job elsewhere. A student activities adviser job might have limited responsibility for a few organizations, or it could be a position with a great deal of breadth and responsibility. Of perhaps greater importance, the entry-level position that seems only marginally attractive, within a less desired office, might in a short time provide a springboard into another more desired position elsewhere on the campus. In short, the value of a position should not be hastily judged by its title.

Once in a position, there are other key factors to consider during those first few weeks on the job. Starting in an exciting new position, the young professional might be eager to prove the worth of recently earned credentials to the rest of the university community. However, the new person probably does not know anything about the *specifics* of the position, the mechanics of the office workings, or the expectations that others have of the new person on the staff. Everything in the campus interview sounded exciting and positive ("broad-based responsibilies, flexibility, room for initiative and creativity") but at 8:00 a.m. on the first day of work there are decisions to make, students to see, meetings to attend, and not much time to orient that new staff member. Whatever the particular case, the new professional *must not wait* to be oriented by others to the new job. Very likely the others in the department will be so consumed by their own work loads that, as much as they would like to take time to provide a thorough orientation, the newcomer will have to take the initiative in becoming acquainted with the system. One's own needs for information must first be defined and then questions asked to find direction. Others will be grateful to the trainee for relieving them of the total burden and in the end the new person will be better filled in with relevant information, at least enough to get started on the immediate tasks at hand.

In addition, the new professional must become acquainted with the reputation of the department. In the interview process, it is difficult to find out how others on campus perceive a particular department and therefore how they might perceive the new staff member as an extension of that department. To a certain degree, an individual inherits the reputation of a department or an institution (Wrenn, 1951). How does that reputation impact the new staff member's role when dealing with other campus offices? What does the individual's title communicate? Has the new person accepted an image which is consistent with personal values and needs or is some clarification needed? One should consider these questions early and gain an understanding of how one "fits in" with the rest of the university.

The First Year: A Time for Exploration and Growth

Well into the first year on the job, most new professionals will feel that there is much to learn and much to accomplish in a new environment. One's professional life is very different from life as a graduate student. Progress and achievement in school were the primary concerns at the time, and one needed to be only minimally attentive to the performance of the department or institution. However, in joining a staff, *what* a staff member does and *how* it is accomplished have an effect on the performance of other colleagues and the department as a whole (Warnath, 1971).

The first year is a time for testing skills that one has brought to the job and a time for learning new skills. In graduate school, a person probably has the opportunity to become an effective communicator, group leader, scholar, and counselor. Now one must also learn to be an effective administrator, supervisor, and manager. It is a time to learn the art of being politically astute in a university environment that is often highly political. It is a time to learn from colleagues and to benefit from their experiences. There is an excitement in formulating important institutional policies and seeing those policies implemented.

Throughout this early period in a career, one learns to build bridges at various levels across diverse populations within the institution. Perhaps of most importance, the new staff member learns how to become an educator. In addition to managing and administering a program, one also works closely with students and is able to confirm the value of personal skills and experiences that are offered to those students. One develops a new professional identity with an array of new skills and competencies that go far beyond the understandings that were evident upon graduation. One experiences the pleasure of growing knowledgeable in a particular area, however small that area might be, and one finds satisfaction in representing this bit of expertise to students and colleagues in other offices.

Unfortunately, all is not quite so positive. The first year is also a time for offering "new" ideas to the department and finding that the ideas are not at all new; they have been offered before by others and have either been deemed inappropriate or have been implemented and proven ineffective. It is a time for developing a high tolerance for ambiguity. The new person yearns for some direct answers to direct questions, but learns that "there just aren't always simple solutions to all of the problems." It becomes all too clear that student affairs tends to be an area that often is reacting to daily problems, and the frustration of not being able to plan as much as one would like can be overwhelming for some individuals.

This is a time, for some, when the watchful eye of a supervisor seems ever present and a subtle sense of continuous evaluation can sometimes negatively affect a person's self-confidence. It can also be a time of loneliness—a feeling that, in terms of age and interests, a young student affairs professional is alone somewhere between the students and the older members of the university staff. The thought of seeing how much beer one can consume at a Greek or residence hall party is not particularly attractive, nor would it do much for a professional reputation.

However, a night on the town with some older colleagues might prove to be considerably less than exciting.

Achieving Competence—and More

The new person on staff, like other staff members, wants to be perceived as doing a competent job. In fact, the pressure may be a little greater for a new staff member, since others will be particularly cognizant of a newcomer's mistakes and accomplishments. Assuming a basic level of competence and an acceptance by colleagues of the new person, what differentiates the "acceptable" employee from the "outstanding" one? How does the perception of the first-year professional change from one of "a solid member of the staff" to "a solid staff member, a leader, and one of the stronger members of the department"? Those who fit this latter category are undoubtedly the staff members who bring enthusiasm and competence to their immediate tasks, but who also reach out beyond their own needs to assist colleagues.

Outstanding staff members are the ones who make it a point to understand the broader issues and concerns of the department and the institution, and who therefore are better able to articulate departmental needs and to understand how their own area fits in with other aspects of the department. They do not fall victim to the sort of tunnel vision that often characterizes the entry-level staff member who can see issues only one way and with a limited understanding of subtle complexities. Perhaps of most importance, the outstanding young professionals are able to *effectively* capitalize on a very basic strength inherent in most first-year people—they *understand* the needs and lifestyles of students and are able to influence policy making because of this understanding.

As administrators move further away from their days in graduate school, there can be a tendency to lose touch with current student thinking. The new staff member is still closely in touch with student lifestyles, and therefore can be a positive force in representing student needs. However, too many young staff members confuse their role as a responsive administrator with that of a pure *advocate* for students. Thus, though their intentions are positive, their eager and adamant stances on student issues may alienate them from the very colleagues who need to hear their message. The truly exceptional first-year person is one who understands and assists students, can articulate student needs while policy formation is in progress and effectively influence others, and maintain a balanced perspective on the issues because of a greater understanding of departmental and institutional management concerns.

Professional Development

Just when a new staff member begins to feel that the job requirements are making sense and the initial orientation is completed, someone may come along to suggest that involvement in a professional organization would be a logical next step in the new person's career development. Thoughts of assuming additional work will probably seem unattractive at the time, but if a supervisor is committed to professional development it is likely that staff members will find themselves reaching beyond the immediate campus for further education.

Objections from the new staff member might rest on arguments related to time constraints, to the belief that professional development can come at a later date when a more thorough understanding of one's job is realized, and to a vague sense that many individuals become committed to professional organizations only for self-serving purposes related to career ladder climbing. These objections may well be warranted. However, counter arguments from a supervisor would probably rely on illustrative examples of prominent student affairs professionals who have contributed significantly to both their individual campuses and the professional organization. In addition, a strong argument could be made for the value of learning about successful programs and *avoiding the risk of having a limited view of the profession*. If nothing else, meeting other people within any professional organization can be productive when a quick phone call to a new acquaintance at another campus can help one gain a different perspective on a common issue.

Once one accepts the idea that professional involvement could be helpful and productive, the next step is to determine how to become involved. If a person does nothing else, joining an appropriate organization is essential in order to receive the professional literature associated with the group. Beyond this first step, decisions must be made about involvement in a variety of available task groups within regional associations, opportunities to attend regional and national meetings, chances to make a workshop presentation at a conference, or opportunities to become involved in the publications that represent the organization.

If one's services are offered, there is a *very* good chance that one will be welcomed and given opportunities for further professional enrichment. Whether the affiliation is with NASPA, APA, ACPA, NAWDAC, ACUHO, or one of the many other organizations, new professionals will generally find that their views of the profession are dramatically broadened beyond the scope of their own campus boundaries. The time to become involved, at least at a minimal level, is during the first year of professional employment.

Realities of Life in Student Affairs

Over the years, many authors have written about the mental health pitfalls in the student personnel profession (Biggs, 1975; Mueller, 1961; Wrenn, 1951). As with most professions that involve a great deal of human interaction, an emotional strain can be associated with university life. One typically finds enjoyment and challenge in this work, but the constant student contact can become very draining. Additionally, the new person on a staff is usually the one who attends night meetings of student government or the many evening programs and social functions that require the presence of an adviser to the particular student organization. The long hours can become a problem, but perhaps a larger concern is that there seems to be little opportunity to see the results of one's work. Students might seek a staff member's help, but seldom does the staff member learn the result of counseling or advice that has been given. The new professional often finds that it becomes all too easy to expect too much of oneself. A disparity exists between student need and the staff member's ability to meet it. If one begins to take oneself too seriously, it is easy to become *too* engrossed in programs, administrative concerns, and student problems. And there are times when the first-year professional feels as if the bottom step of the career ladder is a long, long way from the top of the ladder. One feels a sense of powerlessness, and it would be unrealistic to expect it to be different in the first year.

How a staff member feels about the first year in this profession probably depends as much, if not more, on the person's own personal life as on professional issues. The first year will undoubtedly have its ups and downs. Most staff members will have learned a great deal and also will have contributed positively to their respective departments and institutions. Yet, perhaps of even greater importance, the new professional will have begun to grasp the complexity of establishing personal/professional priorities.

The job is not one's entire life. At least it *should* not be and will not be if one continually seeks quality private time along with time for friends and family. Being a workaholic is no great distinction. No special skill is required, nor should any pride be taken in directing all of one's energies toward a job. It is difficult yet satisfying to know that a good balance has been struck between professional committments and personal needs.

As the first year draws to a close, evaluative thoughts related to one's chosen career eventually surface during welcomed quiet moments. Even amidst the ever-present rumors that increasing numbers of professionals are leaving the student affairs field, a strong core group of young staff members seem to end their first year with a sense of optimism about the future. The first year in any profession will present difficulties (as will every year after that), but the rewards for working in student affairs far outweigh the negative factors. A high value is placed on the close friendships formed with students and staff over the year, and at some point during the summer most staff members find themselves looking forward to the fall, when a new wave of students overtakes the campus. Though results of work with students are not easily quantified or even recognized, when one *is* fortunate enough to see a student's personal, intellectual, or social growth, the satisfaction of such a realization is substantial.

In addition to gaining new skills and refining old ones during the first year of employment, an individual will undoubtedly recognize that a tremendous amount of personal intellectual and emotional growth has taken place. The university setting provides a challenging and exciting atmosphere for the student affairs professional as well as for the student. The first year rushes by as new challenges are met, crises are solved, and a constant assessment of one's own strengths and weaknesses is conducted. Career goals are frequently evaluated and often altered to fit with new understandings of the profession.

At the end of the first year, for many it is a time to relax and perhaps take a needed vacation. Soon it will be time to start all over again, and just as the returning college sophomore feels far older and wiser than the entering freshman, the second-year professional begins the new fall with far greater confidence and conviction than was evident in the first year. It is a good feeling to retain, and the bright, well-balanced and dedicated young professionals will continue to feel good about themselves, the students with whom they work, and the profession they have chosen.

The Middle Management Professional

by Orcilia Z. Forbes, Portland State University

The growth in higher education has been positive and challenging for student affairs. Expanded educational opportunities have attracted a very diverse and exciting student population, and meeting the needs of students has required new methods of delivering services. The nature of services has expanded, the expertise required has increased, and new organizational schemes have emerged. Among the significant administrative changes has been the emergence of a new group of student affairs administrators—the middle managers. For most individuals, moving into a middle management position with broad responsibilities means a shift from a specialist role to a management role. While most student affairs workers have achieved expertise within a professional specialty, they may find themselves working in areas where others have the professional expertise. Therefore, acquiring administrative and planning skills will become essential in order to make the transition to middle management.

The Role of the Middle Management Staff

Typically, as the organization increases in size and complexity, the senior officer becomes more committed to planning and policy making while the implementation of policy is necessarily delegated to others. As the organization grows, the role of the middle manager becomes more important. In some cases, an increase in the number of staff members will necessitate an additional line of supervisors for which the middle manager is responsible. In certain cases, a particular service might work best as a self-contained unit, regardless of size; a Veterans' Affairs Office or a Student Legal Aid Service would be good examples of such units, where a middle manager has been delegated the authority for running the operation.

What other positions might fall under the umbrella grouping of middle management? The following list is certainly subject to a variety of interpretations, depending upon individual campus definitions, but a few middle management titles might include the dean or associate dean of students along with the director or associate director of the following units: (1) Career Development Center; (2) Counseling Center; (3) Residential Life Office; (4) Women's Center; (5) Financial Aid; (6) Student Center; (7) Educational Opportunity Program; (8) Student Services Office; and (9) Registrar/Admissions Office.

There has been a tremendous increase in functions that require supervision by professionals with special skills. Thus, we have the growth in functions, departments, and staffs that has intensified the need for student affairs staff with good management skills. The term "middle management" refers to "group leaders responsible for carrying out and implementing top management decisions. They interpret policies and long-range goals and convert them into instruction, then construct a framework that line supervisors can follow. There is executive responsibility for planning, organizing, budgeting, and authorizing the materials, equipment, personnel, and other facilities needed" (Place and Armstrong, 1975).

There is general agreement that middle managers are the people between the first level of supervisors and the top executive or vice-president. Middle managers are the key to institutional organization. As their role suggests, *they have executive responsibility, they are conduits for information flow, and they have special professional expertise.* As Couch (1979) wrote, ". . .the middle manager has to learn how to exercise influence and gain support, how to get a reasonable share of resources, and how to get cooperation from people even when there is nothing to give in return."

The Challenges of Middle Management

Now that some broad definitions for middle management have been given, what are some of the specific challenges that face middle managers? How is this level of management different from being a line supervisor? What different variables impact management styles? Perhaps one way to begin answering these questions is to describe the middle management position as being a *role in transition.* Most middle managers find themselves constantly moving between an area that requires a narrowly prescribed set of skills and functions and a broader arena that demands a focus on divisional or institutional concerns.

The management styles of middle managers will fluctuate, depending upon the needs of the persons to whom they report and the needs of those employees who report to them. Obviously, some employees require a great deal of structure, nurturance, and direction, while others operate best with more autonomy. In fact, most employees tend to work their way along a learning curve that moves from a high need to independence. The critical task of the middle manager is to determine the developmental level of each employee, consider the constraints placed upon the department by the senior-level student affairs officer, and reach a workable style of management that reflects consideration for both parties.

There is no formula for effective management at the middle management level or at any other level. Often-quoted management styles such as "autocratic," "participative," or "democratic" do not fit *all* people at *all* times. The test for the middle manager is to be consistent but flexible enough in style to adapt to the changing needs of the individual department and the institution in general. Among problems identified by middle management are lack of authority, uncertainties about their decisions, and the contingent nature of their recommendations. At the middle management level, many jobs require skill in relationship with other managers, with higher level executives, and with people from outside the organization. People just moving into middle management probably have limited insights into the nature of these relationships (Couch, 1979). In student affairs this problem can be compounded if one is unable to work effectively with academia.

To insure cooperative relationships with faculty, it is important to be committed to the belief that the basis of the mission of the institution involves teaching, learning, and research; that the faculty represent key resources; and that the classroom, laboratory, and library are the core of this effort. Communicating this value is easy if it is genuinely believed. Without this essential ingredient, faculty will have little in common with student affairs personnel (Appleton, Briggs, and Rhatigan, 1978).

Challenges for Minorities

There are some additional unique challenges for women and members of ethnic minorities in middle management. There is an excellent pool of qualified women in student affairs and there is, therefore, no reason why this should not be reflected in the work force—including middle management positions. In higher education, it is the student affairs area that must showcase its women administrators so that students can see the successful role models.

There is a new emergence of research in the comparison of male and female managers, including work by Donnel and Hall (1980) and Josefowitz (1980). Rather than to report on this type of study, the important thing here is to acknowledge its occurrence, in the hope that certain stereotypes can be put to rest. A number of concerns are more specific to women only because of the recentness of opportunities for women in administrative positions. These concerns include a sense that women lack sponsors or mentors, a general concern that they may not be receiving credit for their work, and, for those who want to combine a career, marriage, and family, there may be little encouragement.

The emergence of educational-opportunity programs in the late 60s did much to increase the number of minorities in academic and student affairs offices. There was an opportunity to recruit staff with experience in general counseling, and in basic skills development, as well as those individuals with administrative skills who came to direct the programs. Members of ethnic minorities became a part of middle management in higher education, particularly in student affairs.

Since the appointments of minority members are often in faculty classifications, these individuals have opportunities to become involved in committee work. One major concern, however, has been that the types of committee assignments are too narrow in scope, often dealing with affirmative action or special programs and not with university curricular planning or budgetary matters. There is also the tendency to ask minority faculty members to provide a high level of support to students. A program director is viewed as a role model, and thus is asked to talk to minority student groups or individuals quite frequently. Still another area of concern is the amount of time that must be devoted to maintaining a liaison with the ethnic community. In summary, a middle manager who is an ethnic minority member has multiple roles and demands placed on him or her. This can result in the stagnation of professional advancement if staff development activities such as research, professional meetings, and publication are not pursued. This is a difficulty that the minority middle manager will face until there is greater participation on the part of minorities in all levels of higher education.

The Effective Manager: From Adequacy to Excellence

There are several key skill areas that any middle manager must have mastered in order to operate at least at an *acceptable* level. Solid writing skills are certainly essential, as is the ability to gather data and organize it into a concise, understandable framework. Too many administrators have good people skills, but do not have the ability to communicate effectively in writing. This weakness becomes particularly detrimental when one is attempting to influence the thinking of others through a written document that is poorly organized and ineffectual because of content or style.

A manager also needs to motivate a staff to reach its collective potential, and to attend to individual motivational problems of employees. One or two disgruntled or apathetic employees can have a devastating effect on office or department morale. Thus, it is the crucial job of the manager to find ways to motivate employees and to provide incentives for good work performance. Some say that there are no unmotivated people, only unmotivated employees. Yet, it is extremely difficult to determine *why* the person loses motivation at work. It is even more difficult to find a solution, when obvious answers such as promotions and pay raises aren't feasible or justified.

A manager must possess good analytical skills in gathering data, making sense of it, and reaching sound conclusions. Being clairvoyant would not hurt when it comes to looking toward future issues and anticipating the needs of one's boss. Assuming that being clairvoyant is expecting a bit much, it *is* important for the middle manager to be sensitive to new trends and to be aware of likely demands from the senior administrative level.

A final and perhaps rather obvious skill area involves the ability to organize, set goals, delegate duties, and follow through on personal tasks. Any good manager or administrator for a departmental unit must be able to perform well in these areas. Effective time management for oneself as well as for the unit employees is critical in reaching objectives for the department.

Given these basic assumptions about required skills for good middle managers, what then distinguishes the "good" manager from a "very good" one? What is the difference between *adequacy* and *excellence?* There are many good middle managers in universities and colleges throughout the country and probably quite a few who are inadequate in their jobs. However, the truly excellent ones stand out rather visibly on their campuses because they demonstrate skills and talents beyond those mentioned already in this chapter. These are the people who are good in their own areas, but who also reach out beyond their units and help provide needed management for the overall department or division. These managers are able to enter the circle of planners at a higher institutional level and temporarily leave behind the day-to-day operational problems and dilemmas that are evident at the local level of management.

Unlike those managers who seem always restricted by their own personal needs and who cannot seem to move beyond the needs of their individual units, the excellent middle managers can shift mental and emotional gears quickly. They move into the higher arena of institutional management and are able to conceptualize and articulate the broad issues. Additionally, they might develop expertise apart from their narrowly defined area of responsibility.

Outside of their own campuses, the outstanding people will reach out to professional associations for professional enrichment to assist them to further understand the complexities of higher education. They will attend higher education conferences when possible and actively pursue reading material that is not solely reflective of student affairs issues, but that instead addresses broad national issues pertinent to other areas in higher education. There *is* a difference between *adequacy* and *excellence*, and this brief description of characteristics only begins to describe that difference.

Preparing for the Future

The student affairs middle manager of the future will be affected primarily by the state of higher education, but technology and societal changes will also influence the manager's role. Most of the modifications will likely be incremental and thus will not cause drastic changes in the required backgrounds of middle managers. The Carnegie Commission report on *Three Thousand Futures* (1980) best depicts the possible future environments of higher education:

> **1.** Enrollments will generally be stable, although they will be affected by an institution's location, programs, and marketing positions.
> **2.** Funding will be shifted increasingly to the student. Fees for service will be the predominant funding for

many auxiliary and Student Affairs functions.
3. Diverse student bodies will be seen, even in small, residential, and rural schools.
4. Delivery of education will more often take place in satellite locations.
5. Increasingly, services required or offered by the university will be contracted or subcontracted to the greater community.

Technologically, the main changes will be in computer applications and in telecommunications. These will have an impact on all of higher education, but not the instructional areas so much as the auxiliary and student services. (The instructional component has always been affected by these changes.) Management and business practices will be most affected. There are also some societal changes that may have an impact on middle managers. There may be wider acceptance, for example, of some of the more flexible working arrangements. Increasing pressures to delay retirement could affect the student composition as well as employment. Energy and transportation policies on national and state levels will also have an impact on higher education.

It seems clear that the middle manager of the future must be very flexible in approaches to solving problems and meeting needs. Budgetary constraints will require innovative approaches to providing services, just as they will require knowledge of different budgeting techniques. Personnel management issues will revolve around such items as flex-time, shared jobs, delayed retirements, and collective bargaining. These are areas middle managers find it hard to address even now. The challenge to perform will continue into the future. With the appropriate participation in professional development and a strong commitment to higher education, the middle management person in student affairs should be well prepared to face the future.

Thoughts on Career Advancement

by Edward E. Birch, University of California, Santa Barbara

The goal of this chapter is to share thoughts in much the same manner as one might share perceptions of the profession with a new staff member. The intent is to look at the job market and describe some of the critical decisions that have to be made by those aspiring to become chief student personnel officers or who seek positions within the upper management group. The intention is not to prescribe a formula for "success" but rather to offer provocative thoughts that should be considered along the way.

These are challenging times in higher education. In some ways one is reminded of the phrase from *A Tale of Two Cities*, where "the best of times and the worst of times" characterized the then current state. While jobs are not as plentiful as they once were and budgets are diminishing, opportunities are better than ever for "good professionals," those who are professionally active and well prepared with sound educational and experiential backgrounds. While this group may be smaller than in the past, it may be better. The commitment seems to be greater, as evidenced by the fact that the new professional persists in the field despite a less-than-positive employment picture. Further, the "perpetual college sophomore" type will have been scared off by the tight job situation, leaving behind realistic and truly committed persons who pursue this line of work because they understand the depth of commitment required and honestly believe they can make a contribution.

The Job Market and the New Professional

The ever-tightening job market and the tendency of employers to be more systematic in their hiring practices will dramatically affect the hiring process. No longer will a Ph.D. automatically ensure a good position, nor will a singular experience in a particular institution. The successful professional of the future may or may not have the Ph.D. and will possess a combination of experiences. Of course, one must be mindful that affirmatve action requirements will continue in the future to significantly influence the marketability of job candidates. These factors represent a dramatic change from the past, when it seemed that being in the right place at the right time, knowing the right person, and possessing the right credentials were the essential, or even the only significant elements required in a job search. Old models just will not work in today's marketplace.

Professionals on the way up experience many concerns and uncertainties as they attempt to reach their goals. Young professionals often ask the question "Must I complete the terminal degree?—Is the Ph.D. necessary?" They seem to be seeking a confirmation of their own feelings; that they really do not have to pursue the degree. When they ask, "Don't you think that practical experiences are more important?" an appropriate response is probably, "It depends."

People need the Ph.D. only if they believe it to be important in enhancing their self-concept and the perception of the job that they can do. Fortunately, today there is a sense of realism associated with our professional work. This was not always the case. This realism brings a sense of honesty to the Ph.D. question. We are now able to say, "If you want the Ph.D. you can get it and should get it, but if you don't, you can accomplish much without it." Twenty years ago there were few doctorates in the administrative ranks. For a president of a large university to find a non-academic administrator with a Ph.D. degree meant a great deal, allegedly because the person could better interface with colleagues in the academic area. Today, with a plethora of Ph.D.s, employers can be more discriminating and evaluate the possible employees on professional merits, not solely on whether they have the terminal degree.

When looking at applicants one must ask whether they will fit into a particular job description, whether the experiences evidenced on a résumé are directly pertinent to the job, and whether the person will have the sensitivities or the personal characteristics necessary for the job. This means that the professional who is sorting out career decisions can make the decision about terminal degrees and the pursuit of additional experiences from a personal perspective specific to *personal needs,* not to misconceptions about the tools needed to get a job. The exception to this of course is the person aspiring to move to the vice-presidential level. The terminal degree continues to be associated with top leadership positions of our institutions.

Career Decisions

One has to wonder why it is that we so fully understand the need for career planning for our students, yet we find it so difficult to apply basic career planning concepts to ourselves and our own career decision making. Each of us, whether young professional or veteran, needs to build a master career plan and update it periodically as our interests change. Thoughtfulness at the time of entrance to the field about where one wants to be in the future is critical. From that point on there is a lockstep sequence of experiences that will lead to the fulfillment of career goals. Without goals one can move forward accumulating a haphazard array of experiences leading nowhere.

Success for the professional in the future will be determined by the degree to which plans are made for success. The job search needs to be consistent with the master career plan. Job candidates should not be distracted by job titles, large salaries, and attractive geographical locations if such factors are not in keeping with long-term goals. The following four key questions should be asked when evaluating a new professional opportunity.

1. What is the relationship of job duties to the overall career plan?

When seriously considering a job, first determine if there is a direct tie between job and career goal. Such a tie will make it impossible to be painted into a corner with extensive experience in one field or area but with no way to move on from that experience to other areas of the career plan.

Many of us started with jobs in housing, an area that provided wonderfully broad experiences. While some chose to stay in housing, others moved to different areas of student personnel work. Some who stayed in housing did so only because it was convenient, not because it was part of an overall master plan. The important point is that staying in housing or in any one field should be a matter of choice and a part of one's career goal, not because it's convenient and perhaps the easiest thing to do. *Every job taken should show a direct relationship with an overall career plan.* Each new job should add something new to one's professional repertoire.

2. What is the quality of the persons to whom one reports?

The whole concept of role modeling comes into play here. When looking at a potential supervisor one is actually selecting a potential mentor, and therefore great care should be taken to ensure that this variable is included in the consideration of a job. With the right supervisor, all kinds of opportunities to explore the field and to better understand the profession become available. Answers can be found to professional questions, and the respected professional can open all kinds of future employment doors.

In testing the potential supervisor, several questions may be asked: "Is this a person who is professionally alert? Is this person someone I can respect? How do others within the profession feel about this person? Is this a person from whom I can really learn and develop as a professional?

3. What is the quality of persons with whom one works?

The corollary to the quality of supervisor question is the quality of one's new colleagues. Ask such questions as, "Are they active? Are they people with whom one can achieve professional growth and development when working side by side on the management team? Can one learn from them and are they respected professionally?" A good amount of time is spent working side by side with professional colleagues on important issues; careful consideration of one's professional colleagues is time very well spent.

4. Does the goodness-of-fit principle apply?

As with students, we grow and develop best when placed in a comfortable environment, one that is stimulating and conducive to professional growth. The notion of having the opportunity to work with, and for, good professionals contributes to the "goodness-of-fit" principle. But there is more to the principle than good working relationships. One needs to feel equally good about the quality of the new environment. Ask such questions as: "Is my new institution one that I can respect? Does it have academic integrity? Does its commitment to students fit with my own philosophy and concerns about student growth and development? Is this a place that rewards quality? Does it continually stimulate and attempt to be better?"

Beyond the formal institutional environment one

needs also to raise serious questions about opportunities for a meaningful personal life. Unfortunately, personal life questions are frequently not deemed to be important as we become consumed totally with professional growth. When we reach the burned-out stage we realize the importance of quality in personal life opportunities. We need to tend to our personal lives in order for the "goodness-of-fit" principle to fully work.

The inclusion of these four questions can be helpful in selecting the right job at the right time. Positions selected on the basis of "right" answers to these questions enable the selection of the next career move to be made on solid ground rather than on factors that may seem important at the time but that contribute little to one's professional goal. Certainly some graduating with master's degrees from student personnel programs will have only one job offer and will therefore not be able to make the kind of comparisons between jobs that allow for the very best possible job to be selected. But no matter the number of job possibilities, *everyone* can at least *assess* even one job offer by means of these four questions.

Regardless of the number of jobs offered, we must ask ourselves about the nature of the job as it fits into our career plan, the people with and for whom we work, and how the institution and community fit with our personal and professional style. Perhaps not all of the answers will come out on the positive side, but at least, through the process of evaluation, the decision eventually made will have been carefully thought through. Also potential problems will have been identified and a plan prepared to address these problems, once in the job.

Up the Proverbial Ladder to Success

Perhaps a more appropriate title for this section would be "Up, Down, or Sideways Along the Proverbial Ladder." Often we can't really tell which way we are going. But again, with a master plan, decisions pertaining to the proverbial ladder are easier. Each step or stage along the way requires an assessment of where we are in relationship to where we want to be, and wariness, of course, of the Peter Principle, which unfortunately does apply to student affairs work!

We sometimes find ourselves being pushed along, up to that so-called "top-level" administrative post that we think we want, when actually we are better prepared and our temperaments and skills are better suited to positions at a much different level. Take the case of the excellent counselor who is known to be good and as a result is being pushed to be the counseling center director. That person may well be a very good counselor but not a good center director. One needs to be careful about jumping too quickly and easily to the next career opportunity without first knowing whether such a jump is in keeping with one's understanding of personal strengths and weaknesses and of professional happiness.

Many of the preceding comments have focused on professionalism from an on-the-job sense, but there is a second aspect to professionalism as well: a person's commitment to the profession. A "professionally alive" person is not only on top of a specific area of expertise but connects as well to a professional association, remembering to keep a balance between campus and professional commitment. While it is important to be active professionally, one needs to be reminded of some of our colleagues who have become overcommitted to their professional association at the expense of the campus and their own students. Fortunately, those who fail to handle this balancing act effectively are few in number. The majority of our profession's leaders are also highly respected on their own campuses. Professional associations deserve our commitment and attention, but the conscientious professional must remember always that the first commitment is to one's own campus, boss, and students!

A comment or two about involvement with a professional society, and what the rewards might be, is perhaps in order. Some might be wary of making "professional contacts" as that phrase rings of something not genuine, and might even suggest a lack of integrity. This sort of limited professional involvement is not being advocated. Rather, the focus here is on such activities as identifying those persons within the profession who are strong leaders and excellent role models. Tie on to their coat-tails. Catch them at the end of their sessions at conferences and chat with them informally outside of meetings, while probing their innermost thoughts. In any profession there are those who are outstanding and those who are mediocre. Student personnel work is no exception. The job of the up and coming, ambitious person is to sort out who the good professionals are and then make the kind of positive contact with them that will stimulate personal and professional growth and development.

Finally, a further mention should be made of balancing one's personal life with professional needs. The "burned out" syndrome seems all too common at times. It is very important that personal goals be associated with any career decision or any career goal. In order to be a good professional, one must have a firm grip on his or her personal life. On the other hand, one needs to be prepared to pay a price associated with upward mobility. And there is a price. *The only way to understand the cost of success is to understand the people who are currently paying it.* The person to whom we report, the persons with whom we report, and the people whom we value in the profession are those who can help us understand this price.

Many student personnel professionals maintain that this field is more demanding than any other field, or that working with students exacts an extraordinary time commitment, level of frustration, or degree of anxiety. All executive jobs are demanding. Yes, many executive jobs pay a higher salary than the student affairs profession. However, we have the opportunity to experience and receive benefits in other ways. Watching a young person grow and develop, being a part of the teaching/learning process, and being associated with an intellectual milieu are but a few of these benefits.

The View from the Top

Arrival at the top or the termination point of one's career plans means that a goal has been accomplished. The question then could be asked, "Have you indeed made it?" There is no answer to this question. Frequently, when student affairs professionals reach their goal they are not at all certain that they want to stay.

The view from the top simply reveals that there is yet another, but higher mountain that needs to be climbed.

If the climber is indeed an ambitious person, then new steps will need to be taken so that the next plateau can be conquered. This will require a rethinking of goals and an establishment of new, long-term career plans. Further, the view from the top requires an understanding that, were one to do it all again, the experiences and opportunities encountered over a new life span probably would be different.

What Will the Future Hold?

What will the profession demand in the future? What is the essence of tomorrow's professionally alive person versus that of today's? These and other questions need to be considered by the new professional. There will always be a place in student affairs work in higher education for the person who is well prepared and who has a strong commitment to institutional management and to students. But the future student affairs professional will need to better understand global issues in higher education and precisely where student affairs fits into this broad institutional picture.

The good student affairs professional of tomorrow will understand the plight of a colleague in academic affairs, in business affairs, and in development. Further, tomorrow's good professional will understand where student affairs will be helpful and where it can fit in—where it must give and where it must take—all in the best interests of the institution. Students are served best when we best serve their institutions. One needs to understand that student affairs is but one part, albeit important, of the academic enterprise, but one cog in a large and always-moving wheel.

The student affairs person of the future will need to exhibit "downward" as well as "upward" sensitivity. Higher education will require managers who understand the need to be attentive to and respond to the needs of staff members as well as their supervisors. The ambitious professional has long been consumed with upward sensitivity. "What does my boss want and how can I please him or her?" Now, as we have more good professionals competing for the fewer available positions in higher education, this same ambitious person had better be well prepared to be sensitive "downward" to the persons on his or her staff. Staff development is critical in this regard. If good staff are recruited it is imperative that they be trained well.

There will be need in the future for people who are risk takers, planners who are attentive to issues, and persons who have a deep appreciation and understanding of the teaching/learning process. These will be professionals who can apply philosophic concepts to program development. The age of the 80s will see many open doors in our institutions of higher education for persons who carefully plan their careers, who know themselves well, who reflect a new breed of professionalism, and who have an ability to manage and accomplish a great deal with fewer and fewer resources.

Once Upon a Time in the West:
One Woman's Path to the Vice Presidency

by Peggy Elder, New Mexico State University

Once upon a time, a college graduate with a degree in English and sociology became a secretary at a medical school in the northwest, where she planned to live and work happily ever after. Three years later, having learned all she wanted to about filing, typing, telephone etiquette, and office decorum, she decided to return to school for a teaching certificate (not knowing what else she could do with a degree in English and sociology) and started looking for ways in which to finance that venture.

At approximately the same time, the departmental chairman suffered a stroke; her boss was appointed to act in his stead, and all the departmental mail was routed across her desk, including advertising openings for residence hall advisers. Having lived alone for the three years since graduating from college, she was not at all sure she would be able to live with fifty other women for a year or so. But she could, and did, for the two years it took her to complete most of the work for a teaching certificate and a master's degree in counseling and educational psychology. (It had become apparent to Elizabeth, early on, that listening to the concerns of adolescent women was more challenging than teaching *Beowulf* to junior high school students, and so she had decided to enter the master's degree program in order to prepare herself to listen professionally, leaving the transition of culture to others.)

At the beginning of the third year she moved from residence hall adviser (RHA) to co-head resident of the 800-student coeducational complex in which she had been an RHA. Thus she combined her fledgling education and counseling experience with the administrative skills she had picked up on the job. Her interest in learning more about administration manifested itself in the courses she chose the following semester, while her interest in counseling decreased precipitously by the end of the first day of her practicum. ("How boring," she thought to herself while listening to her third client. "If only you could get with client number one, I'm sure you could work out all your problems.")

The slowly dawning realization that she really couldn't become a full-time counselor, following so closely her decision to abandon a teaching career, was a bit devastating. However, the delight she found in administration of the residence hall, the people with whom that brought her into contact, and her graduate course work continued to provide the challenge she knew by now she needed in her life.

The master's program in which she was enrolled included an internship option composed of four- to six-week assignments in six different areas of student personnel administration. At the end of that year she was hired, by one of the people with whom she had interned, as the coordinator of the school's freshman orientation program. For the time being, at least, she had avoided making an overt decision.

With master's degree in hand and an exciting professional assignment in a counseling-related area, she lived for a while in a sorority house ("to learn a little bit about that experience") before moving to an apartment overlooking the sparkling Puget Sound. There she could watch the ferries easing in and out of the harbor on a sunny afternoon and the lights of a bright city with

Space Needle coming on in the misty evenings. Sigh. There was even a special person in her life, and she thought once again that she had it made and would really live happily ever after.

But it soon became apparent to Liz that there are just so many different ways to orient students, and that once you find a satisfactory process, the challenge disappears. Although it wasn't exactly boredom that set in, a need to explore different activities and assume greater responsibility became apparent, and she soon started to apply for positions with titles like assistant dean and director. Although a Californian by birth, she was thoroughly enamored of the northwest and had no intention, either, of leaving the area of her special friend, until she realized that her applications, which resulted in only one job interview, were proving unsuccessful.

"Back to the drawing board," she thought. "Am I doomed to repeat these fascinating-job-search-for-new-adventure cycles forever?" She found the possibility disconcerting but an obvious reality that had to be dealt with.

"Well," a colleague suggested, "why not go back to school? You could begin work on a doctorate and still stay in Seattle. Then you would be available for the right position," he concluded. ("Which is due along any moment," she added to herself.)

"You've got to be kidding," she responded. "Me? A doctor? Don't be ridiculous. Doctors know something; I don't know enough to be one."

"But you will when you've completed the program. Anyway, I just suggested that you take some courses. After all, having some post-master's work on your transcript can't hurt."

It seemed reasonable enough, and "taking some courses" was not nearly as terrifying a thought as actually "working on the doctorate." The catch turned out to be that she had taken most of the doctoral courses as a master's student at the university, which meant leaving Seattle, at least for a year or so, while she undertook post-master's work at the other graduate school in the state. (Institutions outside the state were not seriously considered for reasons of finances and location; a decision to move to a small town 300 miles away for "a year or two" was not nearly as traumatic as moving out of the state and thus away from friends, environment, and job boards.)

Terrified the night of her first doctoral course, Liz nevertheless survived the semester, and then the year, quite well. Admitted as a provisional student (she had not taken the Graduate Record Examination or the Miller Analogies Test before the semester started), she quickly became hooked on the program, professors, and peers, and realized before the year was over that she would be doing more than just "taking a few post-master's courses." The course work was not nearly as difficult as she had imagined—with the obvious exception of statistics—and she found the exchange between students and professors, not to mention the encouragement she received from her own instructors, exciting, thought-provoking, and generally satisfying. As she proceeded through the course work, the idea of actually becoming a "doctor" became less absurd, and her morning shower thoughts turned more and more frequently to a review of possible dissertation topics.

Many of those late night quiet moments in that down-by-the-car-wash graduate student apartment were spent sorting through the information and questions she had about herself.

"What do I really do if I finish this degree? Where do I want to do it? Will I be able to do it well?"

She chuckled a little at that, thinking about the question the head of Education had asked her upon applying for the doctoral program in 1968:

"Why does an attractive woman like you want to get the doctorate anyway? You'll just get married . . . "

Well, maybe she would and maybe she wouldn't, but as far as she could tell, that was unrelated to her interest in pursuing the degree. ("Yes," she thought, "I'll get it and do well, with or without a husband.")

In the spring of 1971, with her course work completed and two chapters of her dissertation more or less accepted, she realized that it was time to get back to work. This awakening came after experiencing a severe bout of graduate student depression which resulted in a twenty-five-pound weight gain and the development of a moderately bad attitude. The assistant director of the Placement Center wandered through the carrel area from time to time, reminding graduating or departing students that their facilities were available and encouraging them to establish a credentials file. Elizabeth did so but refused to apply for the associate dean of students position at a small college in eastern Montana that the assistant director kept pushing.

"Montana!" she wailed. "You've got to be kidding. I grew up in Los Angeles. I'm a big city person, and I have to get back to one pretty soon or I'll go crazy. Montana. Billings, Montana. Never."

So she applied for other positions, and was interviewed over the telephone for a dean of women's job at a western university in a relatively big city.

"Good interview," she reported to a colleague, but that was the last she ever heard from them.

As the spring semester drew toward a close, and still no one had called to offer her a position, she swallowed her pride and applied for the Montana job, fearing on the one hand that she might get it, while worrying at the same time, that she might not. She knew that another year in the down-by-the-car-wash graduate student apartment amidst poverty, ice cream cartons, and loneliness would send her back to the counseling center as a client, so she was somewhat relieved when the dean of students called and invited her for an interview. He even met her plane; the city was pretty; the staff members were great; there were a couple of good dinners—and a couple of other good candidates.

So she waited, and wrote a little bit on her dissertation that wasn't very good, and fidgeted, having already moved to Montana in her mind. He called; she went; and assumed broadly based responsibilities.

"I'll take the religious groups if you'll handle the sororities and fraternities," he suggested. She quickly learned from him a professionalism and commitment to excellence she had not encountered before. He became her first real mentor, although three years her junior, and prodded her into completing her dissertation during her first year as the associate dean.

"The chances that it will not be completed increase exponentially each year. Do it," he commanded.

She learned a lot: how to supervise staff members who are

older (gently); how to relate to male students who want to take you out (professionally); how to develop goals (painfully); and evaluate them (seriously). She also learned to think of herself as a professional person who had many things to offer colleagues and students alike and who learned from each of them in return.

It was also her first real exposure to a professional association (NASPA), although during her work in the residence halls she had been a member of ACPA, and as an intern a member of NAWDAC. Those had been paper memberships for the most part, and she had not really learned what a professional association could do for its members.

Because it was close, the dean invited her to attend the national NASPA conference in Denver in 1972. It had been, she had heard, an old boys' club of the first order and was trying very hard to overcome its sexist image. It failed, in her eyes, since the plastic name tag holders were the kind that fit onto a man's sport coat pocket. But the sessions were excellent, and the enthusiasm that many speakers generated for the concept of student development and the important role of student personnel workers in higher education found its way into the heart of the associate dean from Montana.

Having become a doctor in 1972, accompanied by the inevitable sense of invincibility, she educated herself on women's issues in an effort to respond to the expert-on-same role that had been assigned to her by many people in the community. Having done that, she became a natural to assume responsiblity for something called Affirmative Action which, in the parlance of many, was beginning to raise its ugly head. So once again, the associate dean cum affirmative action officer had found a challenging role, dear friends, and a comfortable environment. ("I thought they were deprived because they've never seen a ballet; they think I'm deprived because I've never shown my pig at the county fair.")

A declining enrollment (from 4,000 to 2,700 in three years) resulted in some belt tightening and the elimination of the newly created associate dean position. Montana was nice, and she gave some thought to looking for another job in the area, but by this time she had grown quite fond of administrative tasks in higher education, loved working with the infinite variety of students each year, and really enjoyed the activities that made up her day. No, she would have to find a position in another college or university somewhere. But where? She sent applications to schools she knew something about, in cities in which she thought she might want to live, who were filling a position that she thought would be challenging at a salary she felt would be comfortable.

She was invited to three interviews: one as the chief student personnel officer in a large urban institution in the midwest that had never had a professional student affairs officer; one as an associate dean of students at one of the campuses of the University of California system; and one as the assistant vice-president of student affairs at a medium-sized institution in the southwest. She would have chosen California if she were choosing on the basis of location, and the midwest position on the basis of title (whether they would have chosen her, of course, is another story). But she chose the assistant vice-president's position in the southwest for three reasons: (1) it was a new position, and therefore presented unlimited opportunities; (2) rapport with staff and students had been unusually good for an interview situation; and (3) the institution and the area were healthy and growing.

Lucked out again, it would seem. The vice president did not resemble the dean of students in Montana in any way, so she was once again able to learn new methods of administration and alternate ways of accomplishing goals. She learned some things she decided could not become part of her style but which she found to be educationally valuable, and she was encouraged to become professionally active at first in the regional activites of the National Association of Student Personnel Administration and later on the national level.

The vice president went on educational leave during 1976-77, leaving Liz in charge of the division, a responsibility she assumed with some trepidation but much enthusiasm. The vice-president returned; she reverted to the number two position, returning to the acting job three months later upon his permanent departure. Having had an almost unprecedented chance to practice being vice president for eighteen months, she survived a national search and was appointed to the vice-president's position in December, 1977. Once again she had arrived; a 38-year-old female who had made it, who was liked—and sometimes even loved—by many students and staff, and whose personal friends and acquaintances were numerous.

It should be possible to leave her there, basking in the success she never anticipated and rarely sought, and influencing decisions which would affect the future of the institution and the lives of many students. But that would be misleading, and not very helpful to others looking to Liz for guidance. Getting there wasn't really all that difficult when she actually stopped to think about it. A little curiosity, average intelligence, some flexibility, a need for closure, a lot of luck, and a good sense of humor were the basic ingredients. Staying there turned out to be tougher, it seems, because it is not possible to just "stay" anywhere. So she did a lot of reading about the planning process, goal setting, and organization relationships, and talked to a lot of people about the future of student affairs on that campus and around the country. She established an advisory committee to the vice president to assist in the development of divisional goals. She became deeply involved in NASPA at the national level, as well as in a variety of community projects. Having chosen earlier to move up, she was now in the process of exploring new dimensions and meeting new challenges; in other words, she was now moving out.

And then there was just a suggestion of a mid-life crisis, cleverly disguised as normal events; the death of a friend, a conflict with the board of regents, too much socializing, and just a hint of scandal. ("Me and Ramon? You've got to be kidding; I hardly know the man.") There is a hypothesis, of course, that says women don't know how to handle success, and that they often blow it just when they're about to take it all. Perhaps, perhaps not. The syndrome is probably more easily explained by the twentieth century philosopher, Paul Simon, when he says, "The nearer your destination, the more you're slip-slidin' away." Whether male or female.

Forgotten strengths, which had been cultivated during

days of backpacking, bicycling, reading, meditating, listening, writing, discussing, and growing guided her thoughts and actions as Liz moved quickly to meet the test of professional excellence, proving that resilience and common sense had not been extinguished by years of graduate school and administrivia.

"What are you going to do next?" they asked.

"How much longer do you think you'll stay at the University?"

"I understand you've been nominated for a job in _____."

"What can you possibly see in that little town?" "What keeps you there?" "I thought you were a big city person."

"Well, next semester there is a course in student personnel work to be taught and sexual harassment guidelines to write; student government is working on some exciting projects, and we are finally getting something done in staff development. There are some beautiful mountains that really should be explored, the camera and the piano haven't been touched for a long time, not to mention the community theatre which is always looking for new talent.

"Several agencies in town need people with organizational skills, and there are always things to be written; books and articles, maybe, but letters most of all. Letters to those people who were there when decisions needed to be made and the consequences of those decisions lived with; who have shared, admonished, cared, cajoled, and participated in the difficult journey toward becoming . . . a person."

Life . . . after all, is a much bigger thing for most people than their vocational or professional activities . . .
In addition to learning . . . how to *do* something for society . . . (one) must also learn to *be* someone who can contribute to society other values than purely economic ones (Lloyd-Jones and Smith, 1938).

Summary

Thoughts and a Look to the Future

by Lelia Moore, Pennsylvania State University

By now it should be clear to the reader that the authors and editors of this monograph believe strongly in the past, present, and future of the student personnel profession, are convinced of the profession's central function within higher education, and have some specific suggestions on what the field now needs from its practitioners in the way of skills, a knowledge base, and attitude toward change. The purpose of this chapter is to review the main points of the other chapters and then to focus on several of the needs of the future.

Art Sandeen traces our history and notes the introduction of roles and functions for deans in student affairs, citing the shifts in emphasis on those roles that have occurred as a result of economics, times of war and peace, focuses on the rights of minorities and women, changes in who attends college, and student consumerism. Stimulated by these and other social, political, and economic variables, higher education has experienced a dramatic growth spurt, particularly over the last thirty-five years.

Sandeen comments on the sharp contrast between rapid growth and times of no growth that are ahead for higher education, and observes that the contrast has brought on an understandable concern for the future of the profession. Have we as student affairs professionals reached the end of the road as educators who have something important to offer higher education? Were we merely creations of an opulent time in higher education, when money allowed colleges and universities to provide luxuries that can no longer be afforded?

In response, Sandeen asks us to look at what we know and what we can do. He reminds us of our larger heritage as human-service professionals, and comments that this heritage supplies an optimistic view of our future. We bring to the future the special ability to adapt to the changing needs of students, institutions, and society. We are able to teach others to adapt to change. We provide leadership for institutional change. Our codes of ethics as well as our standards for good practice parallel those of other human-service professionals. Taken in this context, what we do has the understanding and approval of the larger society.

As a word of caution, Sandeen reminds us of the difficulty of filling the roles of manager and producer of change, educator about change, and leader for change. To be in these roles requires that we have perspective on the work we do, that we recognize and accept the inevitability of change within ourselves and in the definition of the work activies we perform. In short, Sandeen suggests that a necessary condition for the student affairs professional of the future is to have a less-than-total ego involvement in work. One's personal life must supply important sources of need satisfaction in order for the student personnel professional to function objectively in the work environment of the future.

Sandeen's optimistic and enthusiastic view of the profession provides the backdrop for the next four chapters. Shaffer, Kirby, Forbes, and Birch offer a chronological look at the education and subsequent career development of a student personnel professional.

In Chapter 2, Bob Shaffer applies his many years of service

to the field in developing a much-needed perspective on graduate education in student personnel. He reiterates the theme of rapid change as a central characteristic of the years to come in higher education, and calls on current practitioners to attend even more closely to questions that ask for demonstrable evidence of the success of our efforts to influence student growth and development.

In commenting on what to look for when selecting a graduate preparation program, Shaffer first reminds us that formal graduate education is only the beginning of a process of education that lasts throughout our professional lives. Like Sandeen, Shaffer sees the powerful changes in higher education as a time of upheaval, and calls our attention to the broader base of our profession in human services as a rich source of stability in unsettling times. His words remind us that rapid change and responding to it will be the concern of the larger society as well as higher education. Our efforts in higher education will be reflected and repeated in other social arenas as we approach the year 2000.

Shaffer notes in particular for higher education that programs that stress change, leadership development, and adaptability will best serve colleges and universities for the future. He then recommends knowledge and skill areas that will be essential tools for this task. Of particular need currently are: (1) knowledge in the areas of technology and its application to student affairs; (2) evaluation theory, approaches, and procedures; and (3) expertise in, rather than familiarity with, the demonstration of the worth of a program, function, or service. In addition, Shaffer recommends that those seeking formal graduate education in student personnel acquire knowledge of the broader context—both campus and community—within which student affairs functions.

It will become even more important to know how a campus subsystem interacts with and influences the greater systems of which it is a part. In making this recommendation, Shaffer stresses the importance of preparing to serve more directly within the greater system. One can no longer function solely as a student activities adviser, interacting exclusively with students, other advisers, and from time to time the dean of students, and expect to survive in the 80s. Shaffer also recommends that preparation for the field include a developmental approach to the study of human nature, a focus on the new professional's own values and personal style, activities that combine learning and doing, opportunity to see the transferability of knowledge and skills to areas beyond student personnel, and opportunity to observe skilled practitioners at work.

The transition from graduate school to one's first professional job is difficult as well as challenging. Alan Kirby addresses some of the issues involved in making that transition, and offers advice on accomplishing the shift smoothly. His sensitive comments about the doubts and fears that go along with looking for a job ring true for many who have experienced being "between opportunities."

For the new employee who has an urgent need to find *any* job, getting an accurate perspective on the first position can be a hard task. For example, the new employee may assume that jobs with similar titles do not vary much from school to school, and thus fail to ask questions that would lead to an understanding of the distinctive features of the positions. Assumptions must be set aside and direct questions asked about responsibilities, flexibility within the position, and quality and reputation of institution and of colleagues.

Learning to ask the right questions is half the challenge of a new position. The other half is learning what to do with "It all depends" as the answer. One should underline and reread Kirby's discussion of the ambiguity of the profession, getting used to delayed gratification in terms of seeing results, feeling powerless, and experiencing the frustration of slow to no change in adapting to the needs of students, staff, and the institution. Here are the primary pitfalls of any human service profession, yet we tend somehow to attribute their presence to our own shortcomings, and we seek to overcome these shortcomings by waging a campaign for our professional self-improvement. The pitfalls remain, of course, we feel that all-too-familiar sense of failure, wonder if we're fit for this line of work, and become a prime candidate for burnout.

Kirby suggests that when we begin to lose sight of the fact that the pitfalls go with the territory, we have two immediate resources available to us to recover clarity. One is to restore personal priorities that were probably set aside as we devoted more time to correcting what we thought were basic flaws in our ability to do quality work. The other is to turn to professional associations for a broader view of the field, for a larger support network of colleagues, and for a fresh perspective on old problems.

Kirby introduced as main themes the need for balance in personal/professional priorities and the importance of becoming involved in professional associations for a broader perspective on the field. Forbes and Birch continue these themes, stressing the centrality of their role in identifying and developing the desire to remain in student personnel and in establishing a sense of purpose for one's own contribution as a professional.

In her chapter on middle management professionals, Orcilia Forbes traces the emergence of middle managers, citing increased size of organization, and the need for certain subsystems to function as self-contained units, as the primary reasons for the development of the role of middle manager. Her definition of a middle manager is clear and concise, and the section on special skills of a middle manager serves as a guide to new professionals in planning for a move to middle management.

As Forbes points out so well, the problems of ambiguity and a sense of powerlessness continue as issues for middle managers. As with new professionals, achieving a broader perspective on the field and restoring personal priorities are the antidote for these familiar pitfalls.

Edward Birch focuses on career advancement, dealing with two central themes in considering advancement. One is the need for a doctorate. An important question for any professional, the decision about a doctorate is faced by most professionals within the first five to eight years of their career. Birch's views on the doctorate are practical and straightforward: if you want to be a dean or vice-president, go for it; otherwise, "It all depends." Ambiguity exists even in the decision for further education!

The second theme is the utility of a plan for one's career, not as a specific step-by-step diagram, but as a general blueprint that expresses long-term goals. Birch's four key questions, to be used when evaluating new opportunities against the long-term plan, sound familiar. Kirby's questions for the new professional come to mind here, particularly in the emphasis on the quality of one's co-workers and supervisors.

In his comments about upward mobility vs. lateral or downward mobility, Birch refers to what has become a primary theme in the career development of the student personnel professional: career direction depends heavily on personal priorities and needs, on what we can do best, and on what we like best to do. There is indeed a fallacy in the idea that success is the same as climbing up the promotional ladder. Birch offers the suggestion that professional contacts with a variety of strong leaders in the field may serve to clarify how personal wants and professional talents can fit together in diverse ways to form career paths.

The first five chapters of this monograph have provided a sort of blueprint for the new professional, one that includes a picture of how the field has evolved to what it is today; some of the knowledge and skill areas that constitute a basic education in the field; ideas and suggestions on entering the field and progressing within it. These thoughts and suggestions blend together in Peggy Elder's chapter. Here is where the "should-be's" of the preceding chapters find application. We see the difficulty in identifying opportunity, the risk involved in making professional moves, the importance of having a flexible career plan, how experience shapes interests, the role of mentors, the unplanned nature of many career decisions, and finally, the importance of adding back into one's life the personal priorities and interests that may have been ignored or minimized. Elder's candor and easy style make for delightful reading. Her main points are both direct and subtle, as the significance of her story increases on a second and third reading. As much as the other chapters may stimulate and challenge the reader, Elder's chapter drives home the purpose of this monograph.

What the Future Brings

The future of student affairs? It all depends. When we view our own future through the eyes of a burned-out skeptic, we see austerity, deprivation, and sometimes even the bread lines of the thirties. Indeed, the Great Depression with all the hardships of that decade is a fitting characterization of this outlook on student affairs. The bleak generalities about higher education flow unchecked, and one must wonder why anyone would want to work in student affairs. There is no persuasive argument against this view, as it is born of burnout, workaholism, and a lack of attention to personal priorities. Do not argue with a burned-out skeptic; instead, confront the attitude by helping him or her to focus on the renewal and regeneration of self.

When we view our own future through the eyes of one who attended to personal *and* professional growth (reread the last three paragraphs of Elder's chapter for some ideas on how), the problems of the profession seem far less grim. Our first step, then, is to develop a healthy attitude about ourselves.

Seen through the eyes of a renewed professional, the field still has problems, but they seem less overpowering. As the authors of this monograph have pointed out, *our primary attitude must be one of adaptability and flexibility.* We need to be able to see the opportunities and alternatives for solving problems in the worst of situations. We need to rethink current problems, experimenting with *new* solutions, finding many means to an end rather than settling for one. We need to stretch our own imaginations to ward off the image some others hold of us as unnecessary and expensive luxuries. We have responded defensively when asked to defend ourselves, and in doing so we have projected an unsure, ill-prepared, and uninformed image. We have to overcome and redifine that image by offering unmistakable proof that the image does not fit.

Along with a frontal attack on our image, we need to turn our attention to predictions for the future of higher education. We seem to have accepted the grim picture painted by the announcement of declining enrollments as though all of higher education will be folding. If we add some other projections, this picture begins to change. First, the Census Bureau tells us that the general U.S. population is shifting from the East to the South and Southwest (Havighurst, 1980). Based on this information, declining enrollments may more appropriately characterize Eastern institutions rather than those in other areas of the country.

A further look at population shifts by age cohort may add another dimension, and we may find that there are areas in the United States where the eighteen-to-twenty-one-year-old population will be replaced by a twenty-five-to-forty-five-year-old population from whom those attending college would be drawn. In general, urban areas are experiencing an outmigration of population to rural areas. This observation suggests that urban schools may feel some added effects of declining enrollments that schools in rural settings do not feel. We also know that the Carnegie Council has suggested that those colleges and universities most likely to survive in the next twenty years are research universities, larger colleges and universities, highly selective liberal arts colleges, and public community colleges (Carnegie Council, 1980). Thus, even though a college or university might be in the East and in an urban area, if it also fits the description of a survivor institution, there may be no declining enrollment at that institution.

The main message here is that specific local and regional projections based on Census Bureau data about numbers, age, and sex of future populations may give far more accurate information to colleges and universities than the more generalized but popularly held predictions. Positions of the future will be dictated partly by local population predictions and partly by general employment trends.

We are already aware of the rapid increase in technology and its utility in information management. The future includes the use of computers in managing human resources ("The search for students," 1981). Training in this technology is expected to become an integral part of future staff training programs. We also know that part-time professional employment is on the rise (*Footnotes to the future*, 1980), as is the use of temporary workers (*Footnotes to the future*, 1981). It also appears that job change and career change will occur more frequently, as the rapid change in job requirements precipitates higher job turnover (*Footnotes to the future*, 1980). *Shifting from one field to another will thus become more acceptable, and fields with a common base of skills will seek alliances to form common labor pools.*

As far as higher education population predictions are concerned, we know that by 2010 (just twenty-seven years from now), college enrollments will be up to what they were in 1978 ("The search for students," 1981). However, many colleges may expect shifts toward an older student, as the over-thirty-five age cohort is expected to be a greater proportion of the population (Havighurst, 1980). Finally, colleges and universities may also look forward to greater pressure to provide education for local employees and volunteer agencies, as communities make an effort to integrate education as a community role (Rutter, 1981).

Changes such as these dictate the need for a broad perspective, one that goes well beyond a single job title or a single office on campus. This broader view and the ability to see how one can fit into and serve the greater campus and local community are essential for our survival over the next few decades. The future of student affairs as a human service profession is alive and vital as ever. Its face may change, but its essential function of managing, supervising, helping, and educating will remain intact and essential. The future is indeed promising.

Selected Bibliography

Appleton, J.R., Briggs, C.M., & Rhatigan, J.J. *Pieces of Eight: The Rites, Roles and Styles of the Dean by Eight Who Have Been There.* Portland, Oregon: National Association of Student Personnel Administrators, 1978.

Arner, T. D., Peterson, W. D., Hawkins, L. T., Arner, C., & Spooner, S. E. Student personnel education: A process-outcome model. *Journal of College Student Personnel*, 1976, *17*, 334-341.

Biggs, D. A., Barnhard, W., & Bakkenish, N. Job attitudes of student personnel workers and their work situations. *Journal of College Student Personnel*, 1975, *16*, 114-118.

Brubacher, J. S., & Rudy, W. *Higher education in transition.* New York: Harper & Row, 1976.

Carnegie Council on Policy Studies in Higher Education. *Three thousand futures: The next twenty years for higher education.* San Francisco: Jossey-Bass, 1980.

Couch, P. Learning to be a middle manager. *Business Horizons*, 1979, *22*, 33-41.

Council of Student Personnel Associations in Higher Education, Commission on Professional Development. *A proposal for professional preparation in college student personnel work.* The Council of Student Personnel Association in Higher Education, 1964.

Council of Student Personnel Associations in Higher Education, Commission on Professional Development. *Student development services in higher education.* The Council of Student Personnel Association in Higher Education, 1975.

Creamer, D. *Student development in higher education* (ACPA Media Publication Number 27). Cincinnati: University of Cincinnati, 1980.

Donnell, S., & Hall, J. Men and women as managers: A significant case of no significant difference. *Organizational Dynamics*, 1980, *6*, 60-77.

Footnotes to the future, 1980, *9* (2), Washington, DC: Futuremics, Inc.

Footnotes to the future. 1980 *9* (8), Washington, DC: Futuremics, Inc.

Footnotes to the future, 1981, *10* (4), Washington, DC: Futuremics, Inc.

Harper, W. R. Scientific study of the college student. In *The Trend in Higher Education*. Chicago: University of Chicago Press, 1950.

Havighurst, R. J. Social and developmental psychology: Trends influencing the future of counseling. *Personnel and Guidance Journal*, 1980, *58* (5), 328-333.

Jones, L. W., & Nowotny, F. A. (Eds.). *Preparing for the new decade*. (New Directions for Higher Education, No. 28.) San Francisco: Jossey-Bass, 1978.

Josefowitz, N. Management men and women: Closed vs. open doors. *Harvard Business Review*, 1980, *58*, 56-58.

Kerr, C. Key issues for higher education in the 1980s. In L.W. Jones & F.A. Nowotny (Eds.), *Preparing for the new decade*. (New Directions for Higher Education, No. 28.) San Francisco: Jossey-Bass, 1979.

Knefelkamp, L., Widick, C., & Parker, C. A. *Applying new developmental findings*. (New Directions for Student Services, No. 4.) San Francisco: Jossey-Bass, 1978.

Knock, G. H. (Ed.). *Perspectives on the preparation of student affairs professionals*. (Student Personnel Series, No. 22.) Washington, DC: American College Personnel Association, 1977.

Leonard, E. A. *Origins of personnel services in American higher education.* New York: McGraw-Hill, 1938.

Lloyd-Jones, E., & Smith, M. R. *A student personnel program for higher education.* New York: McGraw-Hill, 1938.

Mathews, L. K. *The dean of women.* Boston: Houghton Mifflin, 1915.

Miller, T. K., & Carpenter, D. S. Professional preparation for today and tomorrow. In D. Creamer (Ed.), *Student development in higher education.* (ACPA Media Publication Number 27.) Cincinnati: University of Cincinnati, 1980.

Miller, T. K., & Prince, J. S. *The future of student affairs.* San Francisco: Jossey-Bass, 1976.

Mueller, K. H. *Student personnel work in higher education.* Boston: Houghton Mifflin, 1961.

Muirhead, J. H. Mechanizing our higher education. *Journal of Religious Education,* 1910, 5, 334-338.

Peterson, W. D. What the doctor prescribed: A process-outcome approach to student personnel education. In G.H. Knock (Ed.), *Perspectives on the preparation of student affairs professionals.* (Student Personnel Series No. 22.) Washington, DC: American College of Personnel Associations, 1977.

Place, I., & Armstrong, A. *Management careers for women.* Louisville: VGM Career Series, 1975.

Rodgers, R. F. Theories underlying student development. In D. Creamer (Ed.), *Student development in higher education.* (ACPA Media Publication Number 27.) Cincinnati: University of Cincinnati, 1980.

Rutter, L. Strategies for the essential community. *Futurist,* June 1981, pp. 19-28.

The search for students: higher education in the next 20 years. *Futurist*, February 1981, pp. 65-67.

Simon, P. *Slip-slidin' away.* Copyright: Paul Simon, 1977.

The student in higher education. Report of the committee on the student in higher education. New Haven: Hazen Foundation, 1968.

Warnath, C. F. *New myths and old realities.* San Francisco: Jossey-Bass, 1971.

Wrenn, C. G. *Student personnel work in college.* New York: Ronald Press, 1951.